Behind The Wheel™

Tony Stewart

NASCAR Driver

Wayne Anderson

rosen publishing's
rosen central®

New York

*To Leo, my great fortune, for he who finds a
friend finds a treasure*

Published in 2007 by The Rosen Publishing Group, Inc.
29 East 21st Street, New York, NY 10010

First Edition

Library of Congress Cataloging-in-Publication Data

Anderson, Wayne A.
Tony Stewart: NASCAR driver / Wayne A. Anderson.—1st ed.
      p. cm.—(Behind the wheel)
Includes bibliographical references and index.
ISBN-13: 978-1-4042-0984-8
ISBN-10: 1-4042-0984-0 (lib. bdg.)
1. Stewart, Tony, 1971– —Juvenile literature. 2. Stock car drivers—
United States—Biography—Juvenile literature. I. Title. II.
Series: Behind the wheel (Rosen Publishing Group)
GV1032.S743A77 2007
796.72092—dc22
[B]
                                                          2006014311

Manufactured in the United States of America

On the cover: Tony Stewart gets ready for a practice run in prepara-
tion for the Subway Fresh 500 at the Phoenix International Raceway in
Phoenix, Arizona, on April 21, 2006.

4/07

CONTENTS

Chapter **1** *Young Smoke* 4

Chapter **2** *Poster Boy for the IRL* 16

Chapter **3** *Trophies and Tantrums* 25

Chapter **4** *A True Champion* 33

Awards 42

Glossary 43

For More Information 44

For Further Reading 45

Bibliography 46

Index 47

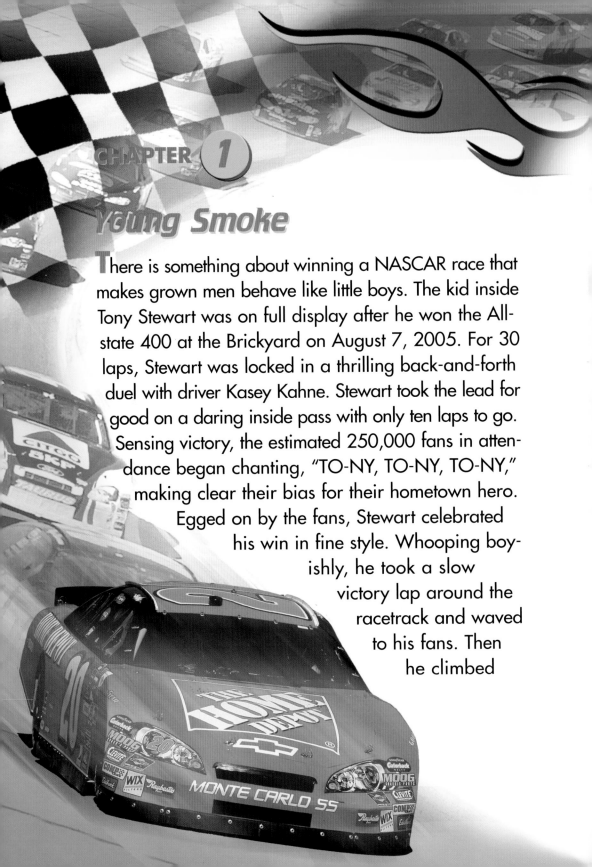

CHAPTER 1

Young Smoke

There is something about winning a NASCAR race that makes grown men behave like little boys. The kid inside Tony Stewart was on full display after he won the All-state 400 at the Brickyard on August 7, 2005. For 30 laps, Stewart was locked in a thrilling back-and-forth duel with driver Kasey Kahne. Stewart took the lead for good on a daring inside pass with only ten laps to go. Sensing victory, the estimated 250,000 fans in attendance began chanting, "TO-NY, TO-NY, TO-NY," making clear their bias for their hometown hero. Egged on by the fans, Stewart celebrated his win in fine style. Whooping boyishly, he took a slow victory lap around the racetrack and waved to his fans. Then he climbed

Tony Stewart has become one of the biggest stars in NASCAR. He owes his success to talent, passion, and a strong work ethic. On September 10, 2005, Stewart drove in the Chevy Rock & Roll 400 at the Richmond International Raceway.

the high catch fence by the flag stand, slapping high fives, until, halfway up, he realized he was too exhausted to make it all the way. He took questions from the press flat on his back, clutching the checkered flag that signaled his victory. He later kissed the signature bricks at the finish

Tony Stewart takes the checkered flag at the Allstate 400 at the Brickyard on August 7, 2005. It was his first win at the famed Indianapolis racetrack. Although he regards this victory as one of his most satisfying, Stewart's biggest dream is to win the Indianapolis 500, which also takes place at the Brickyard.

line of the Indianapolis Motor Speedway, as the Brickyard is officially known.

"I don't want to see the sun set," Stewart told the press, as quoted in *Tony Stewart: 2005 Nextel Champion.* "If I could make this day longer, I'd do it in a heartbeat because this is . . . definitely the greatest day of my life."

It was an important victory for Stewart. It launched him into first place in the standing for NASCAR's Nextel Cup Series, which he eventually won. However, Stewart wasn't celebrating that achievement; he had won many races and championships before. On this day, Stewart was overjoyed about finally achieving a lifelong dream— winning at the Brickyard. The win was the emotional high point in the career of one of America's most successful, and controversial, race car drivers.

A Regular Guy

Anthony Wayne Stewart was born on May 20, 1971, to Nelson and Pam Stewart in Rushville, Indiana, roughly 50 miles (80 kilometers) from the Brickyard. His family moved to Columbus, Indiana, when he was 18 months old. His father was a traveling salesman, and his mother (now Pam Boas) was a receptionist. He has a sister, Natalie, who is two years younger than he is.

Stewart had a happy childhood in Columbus. He was an average kid who enjoyed basketball, video games, and riding his bicycle to the park with his friends. He attended Columbus North High School, where he was an average student who played trombone in the school band and was a member of the civics club.

Anything with Wheels

Many young boys growing up in Indiana are pulled toward one of three activities that define the state: farming, basketball, and auto racing. It didn't take the Stewarts long to figure out what direction their son was headed.

Young Tony was drawn to anything with wheels from the day he was born. He began leafing through car magazines before he could even walk. By the time he was three, he had converted an oval braided rug into a make-believe racetrack for his Matchbox cars. Tony even began racing his tricycle against other neighborhood kids.

An amateur stock car racer himself, Nelson Stewart was so delighted by his son's passion for cars and racing that he bought Tony a go-kart when he was only five years old. It was a yard kart, not suited for racing. "All I wanted to do was to drive it faster and harder," Tony writes in his autobiography, *True Speed: My Racing Life.*

Two years later, Tony's father took him to see a go-kart racing event at a dirt track in Westport, Indiana. There, he secured a ride for Tony in one of the racing karts. Unlike his kart at home, this one had a powerful engine. Nelson Stewart was so impressed by his son's handling of the vehicle that he bought him a racing kart of his own.

8

A Career Is Launched

In 1979, eight-year-old Tony Stewart made his racing debut at the Westport racetrack. He ran the last six races of the season in the four-cycle rookie junior class for eight- to twelve-year-olds, scoring a win and two second-place finishes. He won many more races the following year on his way to becoming the class champion.

With his father as crew chief and mechanic, Stewart spent most of his weekends racing in karting events all over Indiana and throughout the Midwest. By 1983, he was one of the most dominant young racers around. That year, he scored a tremendous upset over the defending champion to win his first major title, the International Karting Federation (IKF) Grand Nationals Championship.

Stewart and his father made a great race team. They worked against incredible odds, often racing teams that were far better equipped. Still, neither liked to place second. Their intensity and Tony's karting skills were beginning to turn heads. One of the first people to take notice was Mark Drismore. Drismore's family owned Comet Kart Sales, which sponsored the young racer as early as the IKF championship. Speaking of the Stewart team, Drismore says in *True Speed*:

> Tony had a lot of heart and a lot of desire, and Nelson was a working-class guy who put in an incredible amount of hours so his son could

continue racing. When you see something like that . . . it makes a soft spot in your heart, so we tried to help them.

However, things weren't always rosy on the Stewart team, and for two weeks in 1986, it seemed that Tony Stewart's racing career would come to an end. Like other teenagers, Stewart sometimes got into trouble for not doing his chores. One day, his father had simply had enough. To punish Stewart for not mowing the lawn, he sold his son's go-kart. As Stewart writes in his autobiography, his father's decision "caused a civil war in the Stewart household." Fortunately, his father eventually decided that the boy had learned his lesson. Perhaps missing the thrill of competition himself, Nelson jumped at the chance to buy his son a used endora kart when it came on the market two weeks later.

This turn of events worked out well for Stewart. Endora karts, which are also known as lay-down karts because of the reclining position of the driver, race at speeds of more than 100 miles per hour (161 km per hour). The new kart was a considerable upgrade over his old one, and it allowed him to race in the World Karting Association's series, which took place at larger, more sophisticated tracks. At 16, Stewart won the 1987 WKA championship.

Stewart's successes took a toll on his family's finances, however. As he explains in *True Speed*:

Karting is a relatively inexpensive way for young people and amateurs to break into auto racing. Like Stewart, many professional race car drivers got their start behind the wheel of a go-kart.

Every step up the ladder meant more exotic equipment and more travel, and even at the karting level that's expensive. By the time I was sixteen, we were out of our league, financially. My parents had spent everything they could . . . but they couldn't go dollar for dollar with some of the wealthy people we competed with.

It didn't help that Stewart's parents divorced around this time, a development that the young racer struggled to accept. Although he lived with his mother, Stewart spent most weekends racing with his father.

In 1988, the Stewarts came to a painful decision: they would sit out the final two-thirds of the season. "We were out of money, buying junk tires, stuff like that," Stewart told *Open Wheel* magazine in March 1996. "I told Dad that if we can't do it right, let's just quit." The harsh reality was that despite his success, Stewart was essentially racing for trophies. Nevertheless, he had developed a bankable reputation as a promising driver and gained invaluable experience that he would later transfer to more powerful cars.

The Training Wheels Come Off

The following year, Stewart and his father decided that the next logical step was to move on to racing three-quarter (TQ) midgets. Midgets are small, open-wheel race cars that come in three sizes: quarter midget (primarily for kids), three-quarter, and midget. Of course, the Stewarts couldn't afford a car of their own, so they set out to convince someone to hire Tony as a driver.

Eventually, they came upon Roy Barker, a veteran race car owner who, according to Stewart, had assembled a nice car but had come up short on cash for some final supplies. Until then, Barker hadn't even heard about Stewart. However, after a few phone calls, he was so impressed by Stewart's reputation that he decided to give

There are many different forms of auto racing, and races are often classified according to the type of car or the racing surface. Among race cars, the main distinction is between open-wheel cars and stock cars.

Open-wheelers are fenderless race cars with wheels that are located outside the main body of the car. They typically have small, open cockpits into which only the driver can fit. Open-wheel racing includes many subcategories that are differentiated by the rules and specifications of the various sanctioning organizations. Examples of open-wheel races include Formula One, sprint cars, midgets, and Indy cars. (The go-kart is a variation of the open-wheel format.)

Stock cars are essentially race cars that have the appearance of regular cars. In terms of racing surfaces, the two main categories are oval racing and road racing. Oval racing refers to races that are held on a racetrack. Road racing most often refers to races on public streets; however, the term also applies to races at tracks that are set up with irregular turns to give the feeling of driving on the road. Other surface categories include off-road racing, like races in the desert, and dirt-track racing, which takes place on unpaved soil tracks.

him a shot. Stewart's father gave Barker $500 to complete the work on the car, with the understanding that Barker would allow Stewart to drive in at least five races.

After two rocky starts, Stewart won his third TQ race at a county fair in Rushville, Indiana, on July 14, 1989, not long after graduating from high school. It was a sweet victory because he not only won the trophy, he also won the heart of Amanda Keaton, who presented him with the trophy. The two dated for five years.

By the end of the year, Stewart had won four races and posted 11 top-ten finishes in 17 starts. Many people were beginning to take notice. Larry Martz, another Indiana racer who owned a TQ and a full midget, was one of them. Martz told *Open Wheel* in May 1996, "That first night I saw him run, I knew there was something different about this kid. He was gonna be great. There just wasn't any doubt."

Stewart raced for Barker throughout 1990, supplementing his meager income with jobs at McDonald's and at a brick and block company. He also ran a few TQ races for Martz. Then things really began to pick up.

Triple Crown

In 1991, Stewart landed a job driving a full midget for Chuck Leary in the United States Auto Club (USAC). Stewart placed tenth in his first USAC race, a national midget feature in Winchester, Indianapolis, on April 7.

However, it was in a series of regional events at the Indianapolis Speedrome that summer that the young racer found his groove. He won his third race there, beating the defending track champion in a 50-lap feature, as well as his fifth race.

Just when it seemed that life couldn't get any better, a USAC sprint car owner named Steve Chrisman asked Stewart to drive for him. Stewart was suddenly in a position where he was juggling different schedules and different cars for the first time in his career. All these races took him to many different types of tracks, and eventually he excelled on all of them. Stewart ran nine races for Chrisman that year, claiming six top-ten finishes. At the end of 1991, he was named the USAC Sprint Car Rookie of the Year.

Over the next three years, Stewart won ten races across USAC's three national divisions: Midgets, Sprint, and Silver Crown. He earned the nickname "Smoke" because he celebrated his frequent wins by spinning his tires to create smoke. With a full racing schedule and deals that gave him between 40 and 50 percent of the purse, he was earning enough money to allow him to quit his odd jobs.

In 1994, Stewart won the national midget championship. The following year, he did something that no one had ever done before: he won all three USAC national championships. In honor of Stewart's accomplishment, the USAC created the Triple Crown award.

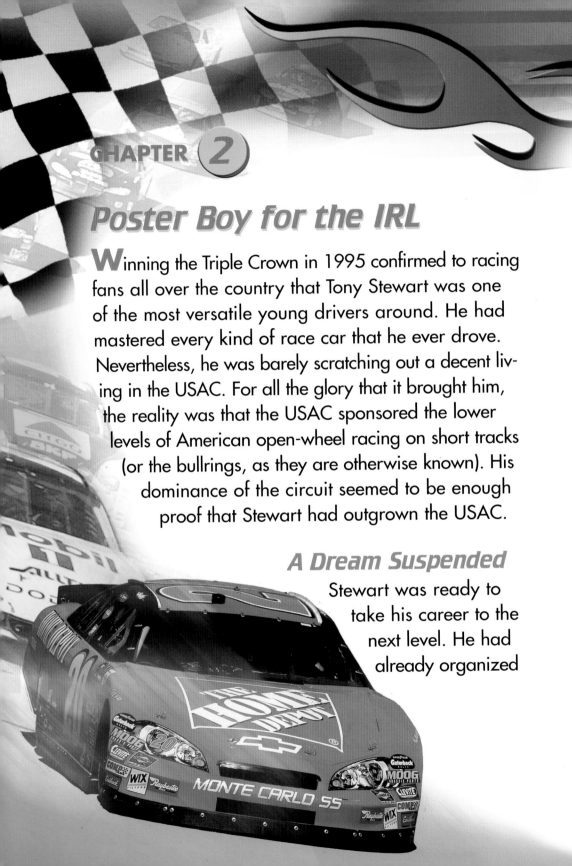

CHAPTER 2

Poster Boy for the IRL

Winning the Triple Crown in 1995 confirmed to racing fans all over the country that Tony Stewart was one of the most versatile young drivers around. He had mastered every kind of race car that he ever drove. Nevertheless, he was barely scratching out a decent living in the USAC. For all the glory that it brought him, the reality was that the USAC sponsored the lower levels of American open-wheel racing on short tracks (or the bullrings, as they are otherwise known). His dominance of the circuit seemed to be enough proof that Stewart had outgrown the USAC.

A Dream Suspended

Stewart was ready to take his career to the next level. He had already organized

Tony Stewart waits to make his qualifying run for the Indianapolis 500 at the Indianapolis Motor Speedway on May 8, 1997. After posting the second-best qualifying time that day, he finished fifth in the actual race.

his racing activities into a business, Tony Stewart Racing, and hired a lawyer to help him with contract negotiations and a public relations representative to promote him. Stewart was convinced that he could hold his own in Indy racing. He especially wanted to win the Indianapolis 500, the most

Many people find it difficult to think of auto racing as a team sport. Although only the driver gets into the car on race day, it very much is. The reality is that the car is as crucial to winning a race as the driver's skill. Even at the lowest levels of auto racing, it takes a team to get the car into optimal shape for the specific racing conditions. Moreover, a race can be won or lost depending on how fast the pit crew makes adjustments during pit stops.

Typically, a racing team includes an owner, a sponsor, a pit crew, and the driver. During his karting days, Tony Stewart's team was basically a two-person operation: him and his father. Today, at the height of his NASCAR career, Stewart's team includes a corporate sponsor, Home Depot; owner Joe Gibbs; and a crew of more than twenty members.

prestigious event on the American racing calendar—a dream he had cultivated since he was a little boy.

At the time, Indy racing was sanctioned by Championship Auto Racing Teams (CART). Under CART, the series was dominated by a few wealthy multicar teams. As a result, many up-and-coming racers were shut out. According to Stewart, by the time he came along, the price of a good ride in the Indianapolis 500 had risen to $2 million. As he writes in *True Speed*, "Unless you had that kind of money, or you could go out and generate that level of sponsorship, you were not going to get to Indianapolis. Period."

Of course, Stewart had neither the money nor the connections, so he resigned himself to reality: "I would have been lucky to scrape together an extra two hundred, let alone two million. So I sort of switched off this lifelong dream, because that was easier than pretending that it might come true."

An Early NASCAR Opportunity

The seeming hopelessness of breaking into Indy racing did not, however, signal a dead end for Stewart's racing career. He recognized that NASCAR represented a way for young oval-track drivers to advance their careers. Having seen other short track racers go on to excel in stock car racing, Stewart was convinced that he, too, could have a bright future in this arena. Most important, he had an agreement with an owner named Harry Ranier to run several races in NASCAR's Busch Series in 1996.

The Rise of an Indy Superstar

Meanwhile, a contentious development within CART promised to open opportunities in Indy car racing for drivers like Stewart. Frustrated by CART's increasing shift away from oval races to road races (races on public streets), Tony George, president of the Indianapolis Motor Speedway, broke away from CART to form the Indy Racing League (IRL). Scheduled to launch in 1996, the IRL would sanction an all-oval racing series that would provide American short track racers a path to the Indianapolis 500. "That was music to my ears," Stewart notes in *True Speed*.

With Ranier's blessing, Stewart's attorney began talking to IRL team owners about hiring Stewart. Several owners, including racing legend A. J. Foyt, were interested. Stewart tested with Foyt, but eventually signed on to race for John Menard. Suddenly, Stewart had a ride in both stock car and Indy car racing.

At the outset, Stewart was supposed to be the Menard team's third-string driver, behind Eddie Cheever and Scott Brayton. Despite his vast karting and USAC experience, Stewart still had a lot to learn about Indy car racing. Indy cars, with their onboard controls, were a lot more sophisticated than the cars he had driven before. Stewart admits that back then, he had never even made a real pit stop before.

Stewart's status on the team quickly changed as the season got under way. Despite not having figured out all the buttons and knobs in his car, he chased down Buzz Calkins to finish a close second in the IRL's inaugural race

The top three qualifiers for the Indianapolis 500, Tony Stewart *(center)*, the late Scott Brayton *(right)*, and Davey Jones *(left)*, pose for photographers at the brick-paved finish line at the Brickyard on May 11, 1996.

at the Disney World Motor Speedway in Orlando, Florida, on January 27, 1996.

It was a spectacular start to a disappointing year. Electrical and engine trouble kept Stewart out of the top ten in his next three races, including the Indianapolis 500, for which he had posted the second-fastest qualifying time. Things weren't going much better in his Busch car. An accident in Las Vegas in September brought an end to a frustrating season.

It was an ugly crash: A blown tire sent his car careening into the retaining wall at about 220 miles (354 km) per hour. "I had never hit anything so hard in my life," Stewart writes in *True Speed*. "My entire left side was

Tony Stewart owns a number of USAC racing teams. One of his drivers, J. J. Yeley, is also his NASCAR Nextel Cup teammate. Yeley won the Triple Crown award while racing for Stewart in the Sprint and Silver Crown divisions.

beaten up: I had a broken collarbone, a fractured pelvis, a fractured hip, and a cracked scapula. I hadn't ever felt that kind of pain in my life." Yet, throughout his hospital stay, Stewart's main concern was how soon he'd be able to race again.

Despite these setbacks, Stewart's season had some high points. He won IRL Rookie of the Year honors and finished the season in eighth place in the championship points standing. A closer look at his racing stats shows that he was more dominant than the final results indicated. For example, he led 165 of the 182 laps he completed at the New Hampshire International Speedway before car trouble knocked him out of that race in August.

Perhaps the most positive thing about the season for Stewart and other short track racers was the success of the IRL itself. It was a great opening season for the fledgling organization, which attracted impressive fan and media attention from the start.

Indy Champion

During the 1996–1997 off-season, Stewart lost his Busch seat with Ranier Racing. Harry Ranier wanted to move to the Winston Cup, NASCAR's premiere series, but Stewart was convinced that neither he nor Ranier Racing was ready for such a leap. Ranier reluctantly moved on without his prized driver. Without a Busch ride, Stewart focused on the IRL championship.

The 1997 season was a banner year for both Stewart and the IRL. In eight races, he scored four poles (wins in qualifying races), one win, and six top-ten finishes. In addition, he led the most laps during the season and earned more than $1 million. By mid-season, the race for the points championship was a thrilling two-man event between Stewart and Davey Hamilton, another former bullring racer, that wasn't decided until the season finale. Tony Stewart emerged as the IRL champion.

In Stewart, the IRL had a true champion. He was the realization of its founder's dream of promoting grassroots oval drivers to the pinnacle of American open-wheel racing. Hailing him as "one of the most exciting Indy car drivers to emerge in the last half-dozen years," a February 1998 article in *Open Wheel* dismissed the IRL-bashers

Tony Stewart has been in a number of serious crashes during his racing career. Here, his car flips over after a collision with Terry Labonte at the Daytona International Speedway on February 18, 2001.

who downplayed Stewart's success as a victory over a weak field: "He has taken the measure of an impressive list of drivers who came in with years of experience in high-speed, rear-engined cars . . . There are a lot of CART miles (Formula One miles too) represented on that list." In short, Tony Stewart was one of the best open-wheel drivers. Period.

Stewart defended his title in 1998 with the same passion and intensity that had won it for him the year before. He finished a close third, only 43 points out of first place. It was his last year of competing in the league's full schedule. He was ready to take on NASCAR's Winston's Cup championship full time.

CHAPTER 3

Trophies and Tantrums

Tony Stewart's exploits in the USAC and the IRL caught the attention of Joe Gibbs. Gibbs was a legendary NFL coach who created a NASCAR team, Joe Gibbs Racing, in 1991. In 1996, Gibbs decided to expand the team, and he identified Stewart as the driver he wanted to do it with. "I loved his attitude and willingness to learn," Gibbs told *Stock Car Racing* magazine in July 1999. "I thought he was very talented."

Gibbs immediately set out to recruit the 25-year-old Stewart, who was still signed to Ranier Racing. He first approached Stewart while the driver was recovering from his crash in Las Vegas in September 1996. Stewart turned him down then because he was still happy with his deal with Harry Ranier.

Several months later, when Gibbs learned that things had soured between Stewart and Ranier, he pursued Stewart across the country for a month until the racer joined his team in April 1997. "He called me every day like clockwork," Stewart told *Stock Car Racing*. "I was impressed with the fact that he was willing to do whatever it took to get hold of me." However, what clinched the deal was Gibbs agreeing to allow Stewart to continue to race in the Indianapolis 500.

An Auspicious Winston Cup Debut

Stewart and Gibbs agreed that the driver would spend two more seasons in the Busch Series before moving to the Winston Cup. After all, Stewart still had much to learn about stock car racing after only one limited and unspectacular season with Ranier.

With his focus on the IRL championship, Stewart ran only five Busch races in 1997. The following year, he had a busier schedule of 22 races. All in all, Stewart's tour of the Busch Series was lackluster. He failed to win a single race in 27 starts. He finished 21st in the standings in 1998, posting five top-five finishes, including two second-place runs.

Although frustrated by his winless showing, Stewart saw a number of positives in his Busch stint. As he told

Tony Stewart autographs a fan's program before racing in the Pepsi 400 at the Michigan International Speedway in Brooklyn, Michigan, on August 22, 1999. Although one of NASCAR's most popular drivers, Stewart has had a stormy relationship with many racing fans. Cheers and jeers combined, he usually gets one of the loudest reactions during driver introductions at NASCAR racing events.

Stock Car Racing in July 1999, "The thing that was exciting about the year was that we ran up front a lot, even though, at the end of the day, the results didn't show up on paper." All in all, Gibbs was satisfied with Stewart's performance. There was nothing in Stewart's record to suggest that he wasn't ready for prime time; nor was there anything there to predict the command

Joe Gibbs made a name for himself as the head coach for the Washington Redskins before he got into auto racing. He has won three Superbowl championships and three NASCAR championships.

performance he would give in 1999, when he moved to the Winston Cup.

Stewart began his first Winston Cup season with a bang. In his brand-new, bright-orange Home Depot # 20 Chevy Monte Carlo, he posted the second-fastest qualifying time at the season's first event, the Daytona 500, in February. Although he finished the race in 28th place, Stewart's qualifying time got the attention of the other drivers, the racing media, and fans.

Stewart also turned heads on May 30 when he ran the Coca-Cola 600 in North Carolina and the Indianapolis 500 on the same day, becoming the third driver to attempt the 1,100-mile (1,770 km) double-header. Unlike the others, he finished both races, posting a record of 1,090 miles (1,754 km)—the most racing miles ever completed by a driver in one day.

It wasn't until September 11, in the 26th of the season's 36 events, that Stewart got his first Winston Cup win at the Chevy Rock & Roll 400 in Richmond, Virginia. However, he closed out the season with two more wins for a total of three, the most ever by a rookie. He also broke another rookie record by finishing fourth in the division's championship points standing. Stewart's success on the track left no doubt that he would win NASCAR's Winston Cup Rookie of the Year Award.

Tony the Terrible

NASCAR is big business. With more than 75 million fans shelling out $2 billion-plus in licensed sales, NASCAR has enough popularity to generate superstars from among its ranks, especially at the Winston Cup (now Nextel Cup) level. NASCAR aggressively courts the media and takes great pains to make sure that the product it presents is as thrilling and accessible to the fans as is possible.

After winning the Rookie of the Year Award, Stewart found himself in the full glare of the national media spotlight. By his own admission, he wasn't ready for it. Insisting that the racetrack is his office, Stewart finds the ever-present journalists and fans in the pit area extremely distracting. He also hates to lose and admits that those

Tony Stewart's combative relationship with the press has earned him the reputation for being NASCAR's bad boy. His reputation for speaking his mind, and his stature in the sport, has made him one of the most sought-after interviews among race car drivers.

occasions are often not the best times for a reporter to be shoving a microphone in his face.

In 2000, Stewart began to develop a reputation as a hothead. He gave a widely publicized interview in May in which he said he was fed up with the hassles of the Winston Cup series. He listed overcrowded garage areas, fans hounding him for autographs, people who tried to control what he said, and constant intrusions into his private life among the things that bothered him most.

(It didn't help that, around 1999, Stewart had moved just outside Charlotte, North Carolina, where the action was all NASCAR, all the time.) Team owner Joe Gibbs wasn't happy with his comments. Neither was Home Depot, nor many of Stewart's fellow drivers. Worse, fans booed him at his next event, and many reporters began criticizing Stewart for being spoiled.

Stewart had difficulty controlling his temper, both on and off the track. He was often seen screaming or gesturing at other drivers, officials, or reporters. Stewart also got into his share of physical scuffles. The year before, in 1999, he was slapped with a $5,000 fine for reaching into another driver's car and shoving him. He has since gotten into several shoving matches with other drivers. In 2001, he slapped a tape recorder from a reporter's hand before kicking it under a truck, and in 2002, he punched two photographers. There were many other instances of Stewart losing his cool, even on the racetrack, where he was cited for overly aggressive driving. He seemed to be always apologizing for and explaining away his volatile public statements and actions. The press labeled him NASCAR's bad boy.

Stewart was forced to admit that he had a problem. His temper tantrums were getting as much attention as his performance on the track. He entered an anger management program and promised racing fans that he would do better.

Strangely enough, Stewart's bad-boy reputation did not affect his racing. It seems that the very passion that spikes his temper also fuels his intensity on the track. He followed his rookie season with a fifth-place finish in the championship points standings in 2000 and a second-place finish in 2001. In 2002, Stewart won his first Winston Cup Championship, remarkably while he was on probation—a first for a NASCAR champion.

It was an incredible championship season and a controversial victory. While no one questioned Stewart's achievements on the racetrack, many sports journalists were uncomfortable with Tony the Terrible, as they referred to him, being NASCAR's new crown prince. Therefore, it came as no surprise that Stewart didn't win the Speed Driver of the Year award, which is decided by a panel of journalists and fan votes. There was also much concern about what kind of champion Stewart would be. Would he be able to control his temper enough to promote the sport in a full slate of public appearances?

Becoming champion—or perhaps the anger management sessions—mellowed Stewart long enough for him to meet those responsibilities without incident. He followed up his winning season with top-ten finishes in 2003 and 2004. As before, his on-track performances were punctuated by his temper tantrums.

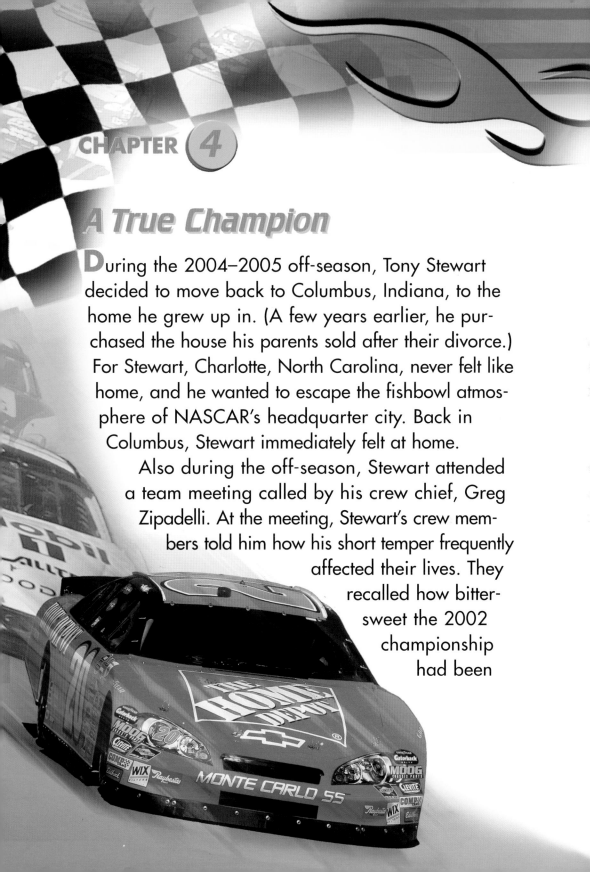

CHAPTER 4

A True Champion

During the 2004–2005 off-season, Tony Stewart decided to move back to Columbus, Indiana, to the home he grew up in. (A few years earlier, he purchased the house his parents sold after their divorce.) For Stewart, Charlotte, North Carolina, never felt like home, and he wanted to escape the fishbowl atmosphere of NASCAR's headquarter city. Back in Columbus, Stewart immediately felt at home.

Also during the off-season, Stewart attended a team meeting called by his crew chief, Greg Zipadelli. At the meeting, Stewart's crew members told him how his short temper frequently affected their lives. They recalled how bittersweet the 2002 championship had been because the team was in turmoil the whole time. Speaking about the meeting, Stewart said, as quoted in *True Speed: 2005 Nextel Cup Champion*, "That was the best thing that happened. I sat down with my race team and let them vent for a day and it was one of the most productive meetings . . . that we've had since I've been there. We got a lot of things out in the air."

The move and the meeting, as well as more anger management sessions, were instrumental in setting Stewart's mind-set going into the 2005 season. Stewart's calm led to improved team chemistry within Joe Gibbs Racing. What followed was one of the most dominating performances in NASCAR history. At the end of the season, Stewart was the Nextel Cup Champion (the championship was renamed after Nextel became its sponsor in 2004). He was also universally hailed as one of the greatest racers ever. This time around, Stewart won NASCAR's Driver of the Year Award.

The Race for the Cup

Stewart began the season with a seventh-place finish at the Daytona 500 on February 20. He would not achieve his first win until the 16th race at the Infineon Raceway in Sonoma, California. However, that win came in an incredible two-month-long stretch of 13 top-ten finishes, including Stewart's emotional triumph at the Brickyard, which shot him to the lead in the points standings. He

Greg Zipadelli *(center)* has been Tony Stewart's crew chief since the driver started racing in NASCAR's highest series in 1998. Their close relationship, the longest active partnership between driver and crew chief in the Nextel Cup Series, has yielded a Rookie of the Year title and two championships. In addition to providing Stewart with reliable cars, Zipadelli is credited with building the team chemistry.

held on to the lead for all but one week for the rest of the season, eventually clinching the championship in the final race.

In all, Stewart earned a record $13,578,168 for his team. In winning his second NASCAR championship, he joined the elite company of only 13 other men to win

more than once. Perhaps just as important, Stewart's reputation improved markedly throughout the year. In short order, he had moved from villain to hero. Sure, there were still flashes of his famous temper. This time around, however, Stewart's performance on the field was what kept him in the headlines.

Off the Track . . . On the Track

When he's not running a NASCAR event or the Indianapolis 500, Stewart spends much of his free time competing in short track races. Car racing is Stewart's favorite hobby. He continues to show up, oftentimes unexpected, at dirt tracks and prominent midget events to mix things up with up-and-coming racers. Even when he's not on the tracks, he plays racing video games. His other hobbies include fishing, bowling, pool, and poker.

At 35 years old, Stewart is still single. Over the years, he has had several girlfriends, but in every case, the demands of his racing career strained the relationship. In 1998, he got engaged to Krista Dwyer, whom he began dating in 1996, with plans to marry her in May 2000.

Tony Stewart climbs the fence to celebrate his win in the Pepsi 400 at the Daytona International Speedway in Daytona, Florida, on July 2, 2005. His Spider-Man act, as the press describes it, is part of Stewart's efforts at improving his relationship with racing fans who have, in the past, criticized him for being surly and aloof.

37

However, they broke off the engagement at the end of 1999. The two continued to date on and off until 2004. They remain friends today and share custody of Stewart's pet monkey, Mojo. He also has a pet tiger, Tangie, and a Chihuahua, Kayle.

Business and Charities

Tony Stewart Racing has grown since Stewart established his business identity in 1995. Today, he is the owner of the Eldora Speedway, a half-mile dirt track in Ohio that he bought in 2004. He is a team owner in the World of Outlaws' sprint car series, as well as in the USAC's three main racing series. He won consecutive owner titles in the Silver Crown division from 2002 through 2004, and in the Sprint division in 2003 and 2004.

In 2003, Stewart, who had long been willing to lend his fame to charities such as Habitat for Humanity, established his own charitable foundation. Run by Stewart's mother, who also oversees his fan club with his sister, the Tony Stewart Foundation aims to raise money to help care for critically ill children. The foundation also provides financial support to the families of race car drivers who have suffered auto-racing injuries.

Full Speed Ahead

As of this writing, Tony Stewart was well on his way to defending his Nextel Cup Championship. In seven-plus

Tony Stewart and his racing team pose in the winner's circle at the Watkins Glen International Raceway in Watkins Glen, New York. Stewart won the Sirius Satellite Radio 400 at the Glen on August 14, 2005.

years, he has established himself as one of America's premier race car drivers. The brash rookie who entered NASCAR's major leagues in 1999 has evolved into a veteran lead driver of Joe Gibbs Racing. He has also

True to his nickname, Tony "Smoke" Stewart performs a victory burnout after clinching the Nextel Cup Championship at the Homestead Miami Speedway in Homestead, Florida, on November 20, 2005. Winning a second NASCAR championship has solidified his place as one of the greatest drivers in American auto racing history.

become one of the most respected authorities on the circuit—someone whose opinions NASCAR officials pay close attention to. He frequently draws comparisons to driver A. J. Foyt for his versatility, car control, and even his prickly temperament.

Stewart's stats are so impressive that he doesn't need to win another race to guarantee a spot in NASCAR's hall of fame. And many racing observers speculate that, having conquered NASCAR, Stewart may soon leave the series or scale down his schedule in search of a victory in the Indianapolis 500. Stewart himself gives no indication that he is ready to leave the scene. So each week, the other 42 drivers in the race set their sights on the aggressively competitive champion. They know that on race day, when he climbs into the car, Stewart's eyes burn with the enthusiasm of the determined little boy who first climbed into a racing go-kart almost 30 years ago.

Awards

1983 International Karting Federation (IKF)
Grand National Champion

1987 World Karting Association (WKA)
National Champion

1991 United States Auto Club (USAC) Rookie
of the Year

1994 USAC National Midget Champion

1995 USAC Triple Crown: National Midget
Champion, National Sprint Champion,
and National Silver Crown Champion

1996 Indy Racing League (IRL) Rookie of the Year

1997 IRL National Champion

1999 NASCAR Winston Cup Rookie of the Year

2002 NASCAR Winston Cup Champion

2005 NASCAR Nextel Cup Champion

Glossary

bullring A small racetrack that measures less than a mile around.

catch fence A high, meshed fence that surrounds oval racetracks to prevent cars and car parts from flying into the crowd in the event of a crash.

checkered flag The black-and-white flag that signals the end of a race.

cockpit The area where the driver sits in a race car.

go-kart A simple, small, four-wheeled motor vehicle with the engine attached to the back.

midget A small but powerful open-wheel race car.

open-wheel Any race car that does not have enclosed wheels.

pit The area inside a racetrack where cars come in for fuel, tire changes, adjustments, and repairs during a race.

pole The time trial or qualifying race that determines the position in which each driver will begin the race. The driver with the best qualifying time begins the race in the inside position of the front row.

retaining wall A concrete wall placed around racetracks to contain cars that ride out of control.

road race An auto race that takes place either on public streets or on a racetrack configured with irregular turns to give the feel of driving on public streets.

short track A racetrack that is less than a mile in length.

For More Information

Indy Racing League
4565 West 16th Street
Indianapolis, IN 46222
(317) 492-6526
Web site: http://www.indycar.com

Joe Gibbs Racing
13415 Reese Boulevard West
Huntersville, NC 28078
(704) 944-5000
Web site: http://www.joegibbsracing.com

Tony Stewart Racing
5644 West 74th Street
Indianapolis, IN 46278
(800) 867-6067
Web site: http://msn.foxsports.com/name/public/NASCAR/
    TonyStewart/Index

United States Auto Club (USAC)
4910 West 16th Street
Speedway, IN 46224
(317) 247-5151
Web site: http://www.usacracing.com

Web Sites

Due to the changing nature of Internet links, Rosen Publishing has
developed an online list of Web sites related to the subject of this book.
This site is updated regularly. Please use this link to access the list:

http://www.rosenlinks.com/bw/tost

For Further Reading

Buckley, James. *NASCAR* (DK Eyewitness Books). New York, NY: DK Children, 2005.

Cain, Woody, and Jason Mitchell. *Legends of NASCAR: Defying Time—Defining Greatness*. Chicago, IL: Triumph Books, 2003.

Grist, Jeff, and Memo Gidley. *Karting: Everything You Need to Know*. St. Paul, MN: Motorbooks International, 2006.

Hunter, Don, and Al Pearce. *The Illustrated History of Stock Car Racing*. St. Paul, MN: Motorbooks International, 1998.

Indianapolis Star, ed. *Tony Stewart: High Octane in the Fast Lane*. Champaign, IL: Sports Publishing L.L.C., 2002.

Kelley, K. C., and Bob Woods. *Young Stars of NASCAR*. Pleasantville, NY: Reader's Digest Children's Books, 2005.

Mitchell, Jason. *Tony Stewart: Driven to Win* (NASCAR Wonder Boy Collector's Series). Chicago, IL: Triumph Books, 2002.

Poole, David. *Tony Stewart: 2005 Nextel Cup Champion*. Champaign, IL: Sports Publishing L.L.C., 2005.

Sexton, Susan. *Karting: Keeping the Rubber Side Down*. Logan, IA: Perfection Learning, 2003.

Sexton, Susan. *Sprint Car Racing: Unleashing the Power*. Logan, IA: Perfection Learning, 2003.

Sexton, Susan. *Stock Car Racing: Running with the Big Boys*. Logan, IA: Perfection Learning, 2003.

Stewart, Mark. *Auto Racing: A History of Fast Cars and Fearless Drivers*. New York, NY: Franklin Watts, 1998.

Stewart, Tony, and Bones Bourcier. *True Speed: My Racing Life*. New York, NY: HarperCollins, 2003.

Woods, Bob. *Pit Pass: Behind the Scenes of NASCAR* (NASCAR Middle Grade Book). Pleasantville, NY: Reader's Digest Children's Books, 2005.

Bibliography

Ballard, Steve. "Stewart Erases Need for Vexing Question." *Indianapolis Star*, August 8, 2005.

Close, John, et al. *Tony Stewart: From Indy Phenom to NASCAR Superstar*. St. Paul, MN: Motorbooks International, 2004.

Dutton, Monte. *Rebel with a Cause: A Season with NASCAR Star Tony Stewart*. Dulles, VA: Brassey's Inc., 2001.

Felix, Ron. "A Conversation with Tony Stewart." *Inside Racing News*, June 30, 2003. Retrieved February 2006 (http://insideracingnews.com/info190.html).

Indianapolis Star, ed. *Tony Stewart: High Octane in the Fast Lane*. Champaign, IL: Sports Publishing L.L.C., 2002.

James, Brant. "Stewart's Big Comfort of Home: Being Home." *St. Petersburg Times*, August 7, 2005. Retrieved February 2006 (http://www.sptimes.com/2005/08/07/Sports/Stewart_s_big_comfort.shtml).

Kravitz, Bob. "A Hoosier Kid's Dream Comes True." *Indianapolis Star*, August 18, 2005.

Martin, Mark. *NASCAR for Dummies*. 2nd ed. Indianapolis, IN: Wiley Publishing, Inc., 2005.

"NASCAR Driver Biographies: Tony Stewart." Racehippie.com. Retrieved February 2006 (http://www.racehippie.com/biographies/article.php?driv=Tony%20Stewart).

Poole, David. *Tony Stewart: 2005 Nextel Cup Champion*. Champaign, IL: Sports Publishing L.L.C., 2005.

Stewart, Tony, and Bones Bourcier. *True Speed: My Racing Life*. New York, NY: HarperCollins, 2003.

"Tony Stewart Plays NASCAR Professor." *Associated Press*, April 14, 2005. Retrieved February 2006 (http://www.msnbc.msn.com/id/7490554/from/RL.2).

William, David. Review of *Tony Stewart: Smoke*. DVD Movie Guide, November 10, 2003. Retrieved February 2006 (http://dvdmg.com/tonystewartsmoke.shtml).

Index

B

Brickyard, 4, 7, 34
bullring, 16, 23
Busch Series, 19, 21, 23, 26

C

Championship Auto Racing Teams
    (CART), 18, 19, 20, 24

D

Daytona 500, 28, 34

F

Formula One, 13, 24

G

Gibbs, Joe, 18, 25, 26, 27, 31,
    34, 39
go-kart, 8, 10, 13, 41

H

Home Depot, 18, 28, 31

I

Indianapolis 500, 17, 19, 20,
    21, 26, 28, 37, 41
Indy Racing League (IRL), 20, 22,
    23, 24, 26

M

midget, 12, 13, 14, 15, 37

N

NASCAR, 4, 7, 18, 19, 23, 24,
    25, 29, 31, 32, 33, 34, 35,
    37, 39, 40, 41
Nextel, 7, 29, 34, 38

O

oval-track racing, 13, 19, 20

R

Ranier, Harry, 19, 20, 23, 26

S

short-track racing, 16, 19, 20,
    22, 37
Silver Crown, 15, 38
Stewart, Nelson, 7, 8, 9, 10
Stewart, Tony
  autobiography, 8, 9, 10
  business ventures, 17, 38
  career setbacks, 10, 12, 19,
    21–22, 25, 30–31
  childhood, 7–9, 41
  finances, 10–11, 12, 14, 15,
    16, 19, 23, 35
  hobbies, 7, 8, 37, 38
  love life, 14, 37–38
  nicknames, 15, 32
  parents' divorce, 11–12, 33
  reputation, 12, 30, 32
  short temper, 31, 32, 33, 40
  start in racing, 8–12, 14–15, 41

titles, 9, 15, 22, 23, 24, 29,
33, 34
wins, 4, 7, 9, 10, 14, 15, 16,
23, 29, 32, 33, 34, 35, 41

T

three-quarter (TQ), 12, 14
Triple Crown, 15, 16
True Speed: My Racing Life, 8, 9,
10, 19, 20, 21, 34

U

United States Auto Club (USAC),
14, 15, 16, 20, 24

W

Winston Cup, 23, 24, 26, 28, 29,
30, 32
World Karting Association
(WKA), 10

About the Author

Wayne Anderson is a writer and editor who lives in New York City. A native of Jamaica, he is a former entertainment editor for the *New York Carib News*, the largest Caribbean American newsweekly in the United States, and the author of several books for young adults. An avid sports fan who tried but failed to make his high school's championship track team, he enjoys watching all kinds of races. In writing this book, he developed a measure of respect for Tony Stewart and a healthy fascination for NASCAR culture.

Photo Credits

Cover, pp. 30, 35, 39 © Rusty Jarrett/Getty Images for NASCAR; p. 1 © Jonathon Ferrey/Getty Images; p. 5 © AP Photo Gerrry Broome; p. 6 © Street Lecka/Getty Images; p. 11 © Alexander Hubrich/zefa/Corbis; p. 17 © Matt Campbell/AFP/Getty Images; p. 21 © Larry Hostetler/AFP/Getty Images; p. 22 © Doug Benc/Getty Images; p. 24 © Reuters/Corbis; p. 27 © Robert Laberge/Allsport/Getty Images; p. 28 © Scott Cunningham/Getty Images; p. 36 © Jeff Gross/Getty Images; p. 40 © Icon SMI/Corbis.

Designer: Gene Mollica